Northumberland Railway
Stat

on old pictu

Georg

1. A postcard of the east end interior of **Newcastle Central** station. To the left can be seen the large clock (made by Potts of Leeds). The locomotive on the right is a North Eastern railway 0-6-0. The card was posted to Whitby in August 1908.

Front cover: A card published by Graham of Morpeth showing **Rothbury** station from the old terminus turntable. The Northumberland Central Railway Company opened the branch line from Scotsgap to Rothbury on 1st November 1870. Passenger services were withdrawn on 13th September 1952, and the branch closed to all traffic in November 1963.

Back cover (top): the Scotswood, Newburn and Wylam Railway was opened on 12th July 1875 as a passenger service, but was mainly used for goods traffic to Armstrong's Elswick Works and Spencer's steelworks at **Newburn**. The station was located at the bottom of Station Road, near Newburn Bridge over the River Tyne. Passenger services ceased on 15th September 1958. This postcard was published by T.H. Dickinson of Gateshead c.1904.
Back cover (bottom): An early card published by Auty of Tynemouth showing **Bardon Mill** station c.1903. The Newcastle-on-Tyne & Carlisle Railway Company line from Hexham to Haydon Brisge opened in 1836. The complete line from Carlisle to Redheugh, Gateshead, was opened on 18th June 1838.

Introduction

Northumberland is the most northerly county in England, bordering Cumbria to the west and County Durham to the south, and a very rural one. Its vast coal-mining industry has almost gone, except for a few open-cast mines still operating.

The county was the birthplace of 'Father of the railways' George Stephenson (1781-1848) at Wylam, and his son Robert Stephenson (1803-59), who was born at Willington Quay.

The first locomotive works in the world (1823) were located at South Street, Forth Banks, Newcastle upon Tyne, between what is now Newcastle Central station and the banks of the River Tyne. They were set up by the 20-year-old Robert Stephenson, along with Edward Pease, Thomas Richardson and Michael Longridge. *Locomotion no. 1* was built at the works in 1825.

This book features a selection of Northumberland railway stations, including some on the East Coast main line from Newcastle to Berwick-upon-Tweed, on the Blyth & Tyne Railway, the Newcastle to Carlisle line, and on many now long gone branch lines. All the postcards used have been taken from my own collection. If your local or favourite station isn't included, that's because I've had to limit the number included for space reasons - or I've never found a picture postcard of it! It is entirely possible that some stations never appeared on a postcard, though the coverage of local publishers was impressive, especially that of Johnston of Gateshead and Collier of Bellingham. Others represented in the book include Auty of Tynemouth, one of the earliest postcard publishers in Britain, and Dickinson of Gateshead. All are acknowledged within the captions, though some cards were produced anonymously.

Many of the Northumberland stations featured in this book closed well before the infamous Dr. Richard Beeching appeared on the railway scene to wield an axe over many services. Beeching has earned a very negative reputation for his extensive railway closure recommendations in the 1960s, but the process of 'rationalisation' was already well under way in the county by then. Many lines had been built primarily to service goods traffic, and running passenger trains did not always make much financial sense. It might seem strange today that stations were a suitable subject for a postcard, but in the first decades of the 20th century, they were an important part of life, the means of travelling more widely, and of sending and receiving mail, newspapers and goods. The village stationmaster was an important figure in the community.

Picture postcards were at the height of their popularity in the 1900-18 period, during which time they were used because most people did not have telephones - or access to photographs of newsworthy events or personalities of the day. A postcard enabled you to send messages to friends or relatives (*" I will be arriving tomorrow by the 1.20 train"*) or show them what was going on in the neighbourhood. Local views enabled people to send pictures of streets and buildings, and an added bonus was that until 1918 postcards could be posted for one halfpenny, half the letter rate. Cards were avidly collected and housed in specially-made albums, filled with examples received from friends or postcards bought from the local shop. Details of publishers are provided in the captions where known.

After 1918, the popularity of postcards fell sharply, and instead of a range of cards portraying a multiplicity of images, viewcards and seaside comics formed the bulk of postcard output. The doubling of the postage rate for cards, increased use of the telephone and more photographic content in newspapers all diminished the use of postards to show local events.

George Nairn
July 2021

Right: railway sub office postmark from Otterburn.

2. 'Oswald' series postcard of **Newcastle** station exterior. The building was designed by John Dobson and opened on 29th August 1850. In this view, Newcastle Corporation tram no. 42 is passing, while lots of Hackney Carriage drivers wearing their long white coats are waiting for business. The large portico was added in 1861. Card posted in September 1910.

3. The first North Eastern Railway train from Newcastle to Benton ran on 29th March 1904, and this postcard published by Andrew Reid, Newcastle, shows the interior of a carriage. It was posted in May 1904. *" What do you think to the new electric trains? Hope by the next time you come through, we will be able to have a ride up to Newcastle in one of them"*. The card was sent to Master J. Dickinson, Seaton Sluice. As well as postcards, Reid published maps and early railway timetables.

4. A panoramic view of the East end of **Newcastle Central** station, taken from the top of the Castle keep. To the left can be seen signal box number one on the gantry, and the track coming in from the High Level Bridge. In the centre are the East Coast main lines and to the right the Tyneside electric trains. This view is often captioned 'the largest railway crossing in the world', but very little track remains today.

5. Exterior view of the remodelled **Whitley Bay** station, designed by William Bell of York and opened in 1910. A young lad is doing a grand cleaning job outside the Cash Fruit Stores. Card published by Johnston of Gateshead and posted at North Shields in January 1913. The station has been operated by the Tyne And Wear Metro since August 1980.

Inset: Whitley Bay railway sub office postmark.

6. Whitley Bay station interior on a card by unknown publisher, posted in 1911. It shows lots of advertising boards from various railway companies, including Great Northern, Lancashire & Yorkshire, and North Eastern. In the picture are the lattice railway bridge and roof structure. The 1910-opened station cost £6,175 and the roofing £5,344.

7. The interior of **Tynemouth** station on a postcard in Johnston's 'Monarch' series. It was posted from SS *Blagdon* at Howdon Dock on 22nd August 1911. The message reads: "*Arrived here Sunday night after a hard time on the railway. Expect to sail tomorrow for Taranto, Italy. Will arrive about 4th September*". SS *Blagdon* was sunk by a German U-boat south of Muckle Flugga off The Shetlands on 9th August 1917. Twelve men, including the captain, were killed.

Today, Tynemouth station is part of the Metro system. It also hosts weekend markets.

8. This postcard, showing **Tynemouth** station in 1904, dates from when the North Tyneside loop was electrified. The third rail system, operating at 600 volts, was supplied by the Newcastle-upon-Tyne Electric Supply Company. The coaches had current collection shoes and were painted cream above the windows and bright red below.

9. Opened in June 1839 as **Howden,** this station was renamed Howden-on-Tyne in December 1875 to prevent confusion with the Yorkshire Howden. Shown on this 'Monarch' series postcard is a typical N.E.R.footbridge, which is now at Goathland station on the North Yorkshire Moors Railway. 'Monarch' series postcard by Johnston.

10. A Tyneside electric train approaches **Backworth** station. The line was electrified in 1904 as the Tyneside Electric route, aiming to compete with the new electric tram services in the area. The photo on Johnston's 'Monarch' series postcard was taken looking north-east. Backworth station closed to passengers in June 1977.

11. Cramlington station opened on 1st March 1847. 'Monarch' series postcard that was posted during World War One to a soldier at Alnwick. This railway station is still open today, used by 107,800 passengers in 2018-19.

12. The derailment of the Scotch express between Annitsford and Cramlington on 10th May 1926, during the General Strike. 'The Flying Scotsman', hauled by A3 class locomotive no. 2565 *Merry Hampton*, came to grief because a section of track had been removed. Eight miners were subsequently sentenced to penal servitude.

13. Blyth's first railway station was opened on 3rd March 1847, but replaced in a new location in 1867. This Johnston-published 'Monarch' series postcard shows the later station, constructed by the North Eastern Railway from 1894-6 at a cost of £20,000. Despite being next to a through line, this was actually a terminus. The station closed to passengers in November 1964 and was demolished in 1972.

14. Bebside station, seen here on another 'Monarch' series postcard, was in the heart of Northumberland's east coast mining area, which at one time comprised over 50 collieries. The stationmaster and staff posed for this photograph, and this particular postcard was posted with a Bedlington Colliery postmark and sent to Bermondsey, London, in 1910. Bebside station closed in November 1964.

15. Passengers await the arrival of a train at **Ashington** station, first opened by the Blyth and Tyne Railway in 1878 as Hirst (for Ashington). It was renamed in 1889. The station, on the branch from Bedlington to Newbiggin, which had 20 stopping passenger trains in each direction daily in 1910, closed to passengers in November 1964 and all that remain today from this postcard picture are the platforms. Proposals for the re-instatement of trains from Newcastle are ongoing. 'Monarch series' card, posted in 1920.

16. Published in the 'Lindsay' series (based at Linden Street, Newcastle), this postcard shows the terminus station at **Newbiggin** (sometimes referred to as Newbiggin-on-Sea).The station opened in 1872 on the Blyth and Tyne Railway, and closed on 2nd November 1964.

17. Kenton station was opened on 1st June 1905, and initially ten passenger trains in each direction stopped daily, four on Sundays. It was renamed Kenton Bank in July 1923, but just six years later, it was closed to passengers. This station was demolished in 1973 and replaced in 1981 by Bankfoot Metro station. In 1991, the line was extended to Newcastle Airport. Card posted to an address at Hamsterley Colliery in 1907.

18. A classy real photographic postcard of the first passenger train at **Ponteland** station on 1st June 1905. The card was posted from there three weeks later, sent to Mrs Stephenson, Darlington. *" I am sending PC to let you see that we have really got the troin to P. at last".* The Ponteland Light Railway, authorised in 1899, ran from Gosforth to Ponteland, with an extra line to Darras Hall, the 'garden city'. The whole operation was short-lived: the line closed to passengers on 17th June 1929 after a poor take-up. Goods traffic continued until November 1967.

19. The station at **West Gosforth** was on the Ponteland and Darras Hall branch, and also closed in 1929 to passenger traffic. The line remained open for goods traffic from the ICI works and Rowntree's factory until 1989. The site now has the Regent Centre Metro station, opened on 10th May 1981. Card published in the 'Old Reliable' series, Newcastle.

20. Stocksfield station served (and still does) the villages of Stocksfield, Bywell and Newton. This card was posted in August 1911, sent to Winchester in Hampshire. The origianl single-storey house can be seen separated from later platforms by the goods sidings. The station's 2018-19 passenger usage was just under 60,000.

21. Railway staff and passengers pose for this postcard by unidentified publisher of **Riding Mill** station. This line was one of the earliest passenger railways in the country, opening in 1838, and is still a popular commuter service to Newcastle and the Metro Shopping Centre in Gateshead.

22. A rare postcard of the interior of **Hexham** station from the Locomotive Publishing Co., based in London. Passenger trains between here and Blaydon began on 9th March 1835, and the station also served a branch line to Allendale and the Border Counties Railway. Hexham is still a very busy station on the Newcastle to Carlisle line.

23. Langley station was on the Hexham to Allendale branch line, which closed to passengers in September 1930. Here the stationmaster and passengers pose for an unattributed photographer. This card was posted at Alston in 1914, when only three passenger trains called daily in each direction. Past the road bridge can be seen a second bridge which carried the 4ft diameter flue from Langley lead works to the top of the nearby hill.

24. Another Johnston 'Monarch' series postcard, showing **Allendale** station (originally called Catton Road when it opened in 1869, as the line was intended to run to Allendale town and Allanheads - that never happened). On this card, NER class F8 2-4-2T no. 423 (built in 1889) arrives with a train from Hexham. Could the gentleman on the left at the front be about to play a round of golf in Hexham?

Inset: Allendale railway sub office postmark.

25. Fourstones, a typical NER twin pavilion style station, built for £880 and opened in 1880 to replace a previous building. The main traffic here was from the nearby colliery, lime works, quarries and paper mills. The station closed to passengers in January 1967.

26. A Johnston-published postcard of **Haltwhistle** station looking east. In the background is the viaduct carrying the Alston branch across the South Tyne river. Plenty of action on this scene - note the cattle trucks have lime-washed bases. The station is still operational.

27. Coanwood station on the Haltwhistle to Alston line opened in 1852. The station served the nearby coalmining and quarrying communities. The wooden station was erected in 1877-8 at a cost of £670. It closed to passengers in May 1976. Card posted at Coanwood in August 1909.

28. Lambley station on the Haltwhistle-Alston line features here on a postcard from Gibson of Gateshead, and posted in July 1906, sent to Miss Hall in Slaggyford.. *" My father can't possibly come on Sunday as we have company coming this weekend, but he will try and come the Sunday following. Hope you are having a grand time. S. Nicholson, the Vicarage".* The picture shows the signals for the junction with the line to Lambley Colliery and the main line over Lambley viaduct to Alston. The line closed to passengers in 1976, but a section from Alston to Slaggyford has been opened as the 2-ft narrow-gauge South Tynedale Railway.

29. A rare postcard view of **Slaggyford** station and signal box. The stationmaster's house was on the other side of the line, opposite the signal box. The timber-built station, screened by trees and shrubs that gave a small amount of protection from wild winters, was put up c.1890. At the moment, this is the end of the line on the South Tynedale railway from Alston.

30. Wall station, opened in April 1858, was another Northumberland station some way from the village it served, in this case a mile and a half. During the 1940s the main building was destroyed by fire. The station closed to passengers and goods in September 1955, and one of the buildings is now a private residence. 'Monarch' series postcard.

31. Chollerford station, seen here on a postcard sent to Newcastle in August 1911, opened on 5th April 1858, though its name was changed to Humshaugh in August 1919 to avoid confusion with its neighbouring station Chollerton. The siding to the left served a cattle dock behind the goods dock. The station closed to passengers on 15th October 1956 and is now a private residence.

32. Richardson & Co. of Hexham published this postcard of **Barrasford** station on the Borders County Railway. It closed to passengers on 15th October 1956 and completely two years later. This card was posted at Hexham in July 1912 and sent to an address in Cullercoats: *" Just a card to let you know I am sending your coat by post. I expect you will get it by Monday. In haste"*.

33. A view of **Wark** station looking towards Barrasford on a postcard published by W.P. Collier and posted to Benwell in June 1912. *" It is fine weather and I am enjoying myself"*. The station was closed to passengers on 15th October 1956.

34. A card published by Collier and posted at Bellingham in September 1924 provides a panoramic view of **Reedsmouth** station (popularly called Reedsmouth Junction). The picture shows the later signal box that replaced a single-storey one. The track on the left is the old North British line to Hawick, and the one on the right past the large water tank is headed for Morpeth via Scotsgap.

35. Bellingham railway station on a card published by H.G. Thompson of Newcastle and posted to Preston in September 1908. The railway from west of Hexham to Riccarton Junction, opened in 1861, joined the 'Waverley' route north. In September 1926 the suffix 'North Tyne' was added to the station name to avoid confusion with Bellingham on the Southern Railway. The station closed in November 1963, but now an excellent museum, heritage centre and tea rooms stand in the station yard. The museum contains a mock-up of local photographer and postcard publisher W.P. Collier's studios.

36. Ladies waiting for the Reedsmouth train, hauled by J36 class engine no. 789 at **Tarset** station on a postcard published by J. Fairlamb of Greenhaugh. Tarset closed to passengers in October 1956 and is now a private residence.

37. The station house and signal box at **Falstone** on a postcard from Collier of Bellingham. The photo was taken from Falstone village. Most of the surrounding area is part of the large Kielder Forest and Kielder Water.

38. Kielder station on a Collier-published postcard that was posted at Hawick in October 1932. The station opened in January 1862 and changed its name to Kielder Forest in October 1948. The new village was built for forestry workers in the 1920s. Kielder closed to passengers in October 1956 and now lies beneath Kielder Water.

39. Stannington was opened as Netherton station in March 1847 and acquired the former name in January 1892. It lies two miles north-east of the village and is separated from it by the A1 road. The level crossing on the road to Netherton still crosses the East Coast main line. Stannington closed to passengers in September 1958; the station house is today a private residence.

40. Morpeth station looking north on the East Coast main line. Designed by Benjamin Green in the Scottish baronial style, it opened in 1847. The 90-degree curve south of the station has been the scene of several serious accidents. Card posted at Morpeth in November 1905 to Miss Cassidy at Finlay's tobacco stall on North Shields railway station.

41. Meldon station, substantially built with local stone, was on the Wansbeck Valley route from Morpeth to Scotsgap. There was just one platform on the north side and to reach the other side passengers had to cross the road bridge. This postcard was posted to a Bellingham address in May 1906, the stamp cancelled with an Edinburgh & Newcastle sorting carriage postmark.

42. Scotsgap station showing staff alongside North British Drummond locomotive no. 72 (originally named *Morpeth*). The station served the villages of Scotsgap and Cambo, and was an important junction for the line from Morpeth to Reedsmouth Junction and beyond, as well as the branch line to Rothbury. The station closed to passengers in September 1952 and to all traffic in October 1966.

43. The Royal Field Artillery arrive at **Woodburn** station en route to the nearby military camps and ranges. The train was also composed of lime-washed cattle trucks carrying agricultural freight. The station closed to passengers in September 1952 and to freight in October 1966, though the building is now a private residence. Card posted in April 1915.

44. Pegswood station, with the colliery behind, on a Johnstone 'Monarch' series postcard posted in August 1919. The station offices and clock were located on the overbridge.

45. Pegswood station office interior on a postcard from Lawson of Pegswood. This very rare item shows a typical North Eastern Railway office with ticket boards, weighing machine, and a very proud stationmaster. The station is still open despite several attempts to close it.

46. This early postcard of **Longhirst** station, published by Gibson & Co. of Gateshead, was posted at Morpeth in May 1904, sent to South Shields. The station building, erected in 1847, was on the down platform, while the up platform had a well-built waiting room. The station closed in October 1951, but the buildings are now private residences.

47. Widdrington station on a postcard in the 'Graham' series. *" Another for your collection"*, wrote Tom to his sister Sarah at Gosforth. The station opened on the East Coast main line in 1847 and still has a very limited passenger service, but goods traffic ceased there in 1964.

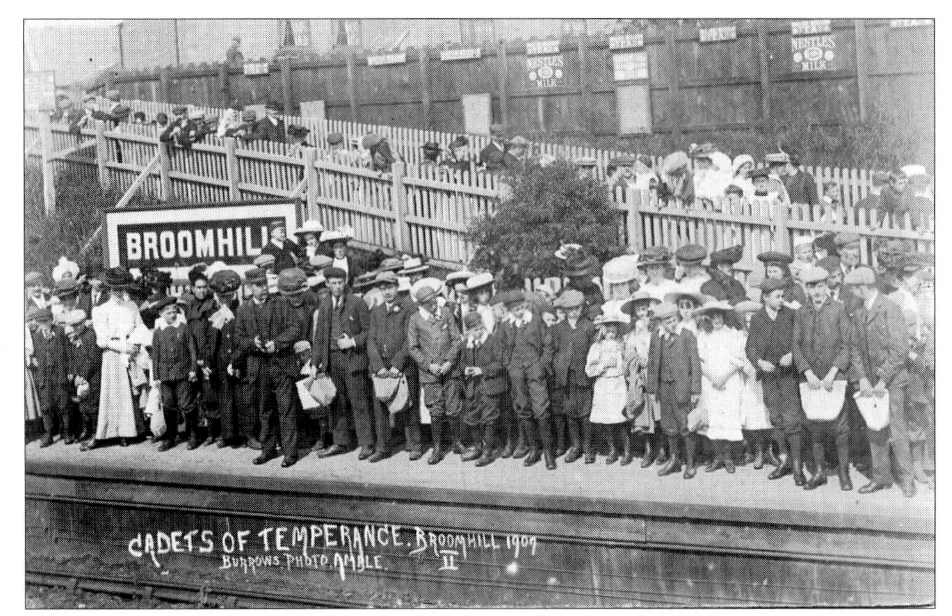

48. Broomhill station on a card from local photographer Burrows of Amble. The card was posted on 13th July 1907 and shows Temperance Movement cadets waiting for the train to Amble. The stationmaster is on the platform edge, trying to keep the crowds back. *" As promised, I send you no. 1 of the 3 ppcs group of the Cadet trip last Sat"*.

49. 'Monarch' series postcard of **Acklington** station, the photo taken from the road bridge, showing the station (which opened in July 1847), goods yard and auction mart. Goods traffic ceased in September 1966, but the station still has a limited passenger service.

50. A postcard of **Warkworth** station posted in August 1916. The platforms originally faced one another, but by 1897 the down platform had been moved a little north. Like many Northumberland stations, it was some distance from the village it served - in this case, a mile and a half. It closed to passengers in 1958 and still exists as a private residence.

51. A rare postcard of Alnmouth North signal box, controlling part of the East Coast main line. It opened in 1847, three years earlier than the station, and is still used today. The branch line to Alnwick opened in 1850 and closed in 1968.

52. Published by Ruddock of Alnwick, this postcard shows the Prince and Princess of Wales's (the future George V and Queen Mary) visit to Alnwick in 1908. Floral arches and decorations festooned the town from the station to Alnwick Castle. The terminus station closed in 1968 and now contains the Barter Bookshop. A recent Alnwick Lionheart station lies to the east of the A1 Alnwick bypass, and is part of the Aln Valley Heritage Railway which will shortly be extended to Alnmouth.

53. Glanton station, well away from the village, was opened on 5th September 1887. This postcard, published by Gibson of Gateshead, was posted from Glanton in December 1905, sent to East Lilburn: "*Got your nice pc yesterday morning*". The station closed to passengers in September 1930. The weigh cabin and weighbridge can now be seen at the entrance to the goods yard at the North of England Open Air Museum at Beamish, Co. Durham.

54. Hedgeley was a large country station built thanks to the influence of local landowner Captain R. Carr-Ellison, and as a result was sited here rather than nearer its neighbouring village, Powburn. The station closed to passengers in 1930. This postcard was posted in August 1908 to Miss Dodds at the Granby Inn, Long Framlington. *" I saw Willie Chapman at Whickham painting. He was asking for you"*.

55. A North Eastern Railway employee stands proudly for an unknown photographer on this postcard of **Wooperton** station on the Alnwick to Cornhill line, opened on 5th September 1887 and closed to passengers as early as September 1930. Goods traffic still used the station until 1954. Note the floral displays - most country stations prided themselves on these.

56. Ilderton station on a real photographic postcard from an unknown publisher that was posted from Whittingham to Dundee in June 1913. The station opened on 5th September 1887 and closed to passengers that month in 1930. This fine building has had many uses since then, as a small post office and shop, as a garage where vintage cars were repaired, and as the 'Station House Restaurant' in the 1990s. It is now a private residence.

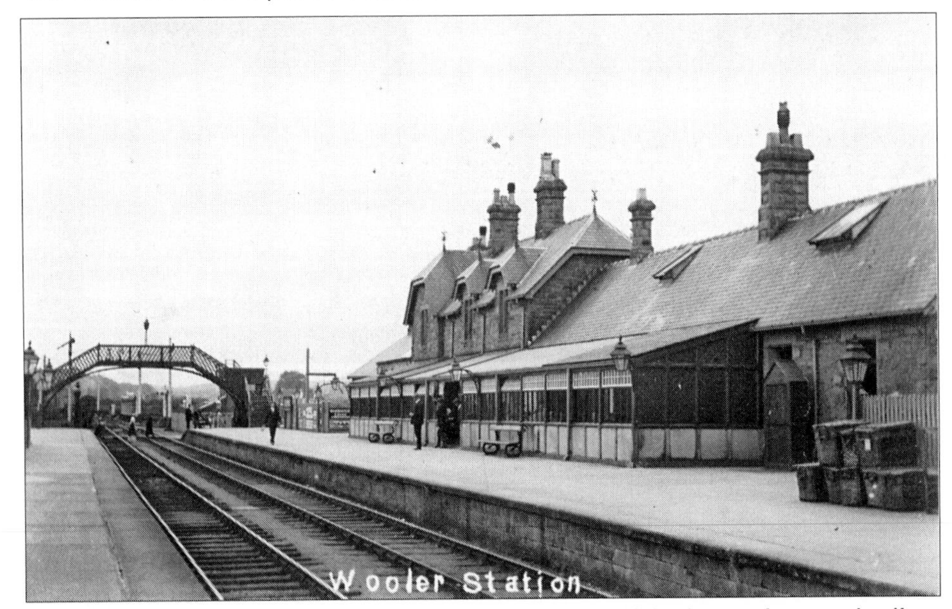

57. This excellent real photographic postcard shows **Wooler** station on the line from Alnwick to Coldstream. It had a large goods yard, goods shed and coal drops. Wooler was the only station on the line with two separated platforms and waiting rooms, connected by a typical footbridge. The station closed to passengers on 22nd September 1930.

58. Kirknewton looking east. This postcard shows the signal box on the platform, and the station building incorporating the stationmaster's house. The final passenger service between Alnwick and Coldstream ran on 22nd September 1930, only 43 years after the line was opened.

59. Station staff pose outside **Mindrum** (also the location of the local post office) on this c.1904 postcard published by Gibson & Co. of Gateshead. Mindrum was on the Alnwick to Cornhill line that closed to passengers in September 1930. Goods traffic continued until March 1965.

60. The stationmaster and his staff pose for the camera at **Longhoughton** station on the East Coast main line. This Gibson-published postcard was posted at Lesbury in October 1905. The station opened in 1847, but like others in the area closed during World War Two. It re-opened in October 1946 due to its convenience for R.A.F. personnel and for excursion trains, but closed for passenger and goods traffic in June 1962..

61. Christon Bank station opened in 1847, closed to passengers during WWII, and finally succumbed in 1958 (goods continued until 1965). The station buildings (which cost £1,135) were typical of the Newcastle to Berwick style, with two facing platforms. Note the two sets of quadruple chimney stacks at this and the one above. The building is still standing as a private residence. Card published by E. Pouteau, Grays Inn Road, King's Cross, London.

62. Chathill station on the East Coast main line today serves the villages of Bamburgh, Belford, Embleton and Seahouses. At the north end of the station was a bay that served the North Sunderland Railway to the fishing village of Seahouses from 1898 to 1951. Today there is a very limited passenger service at Chathill.

63. Satirical artist Martin Anderson (Cynicus) from Dundee not only drew cartoons but published postcards, including many with a political slant. This design is found with lots of different place-name overprints, a ploy that boosted local sales. This card was posted at Seahouses in August 1925. *" Dear Uncle Tom. I have been to Bamburgh today and are going home on this little train. With love, Muriel".*

64. Seahouses station on the North Sunderland Railway opened in 1898, connecting the fishing village with the main line at Chathill. The locomotive *Bamburgh*, built by Manning Wardle of Leeds, is ready to set off on its four-mile journey with two ex-North Eastern Railway coaches. The station closed in 1951, and the location is now Seahouses' main car park. 'Monarch' series postcard from Johnstone.

65. A later 'Monarch' series postcard, posted from **Seahouses** in June 1936, showing Armstrong-Whitworth diesel electric locomotive *The Lady Armstrong* (built 1934, scrapped 1947). Two of this type survive on the Tanfield Railway in County Durham. What a wonderful tourist attraction this line would be today had it survived.

66. Lucker station, built in fine Jacobean style that would have graced a station serving a much larger community. As it was, Lucker village, a mile and a half away near Bamburgh, was only a small place. Note the sign to the left of the entrance advertising a public weighbridge. The station here opened on 29th March 1847 and finally closed to passengers in February 1953, after a temporary closure during the war. Sadly, this wonderful building was demolished in the summer of 1960. Card posted in September 1915.

67. Belford station looking south on a 'Monarch' series postcard, posted in June 1922. Hilda sent this to her mother in Alnwick. *" I am getting on allright. Tell Mr E. I will write to him but I can't be bothered today. Keep this pc for me & all the newspapers especially the Sunday ones"*. All that remains from this photo is the station house on the right, now a private residence. The original Newcastle and Berwick railway opened in 1847 and closed to passengers in January 1968. Several unsuccessful attempts have been made to re-open the station since.

68. Beal railway station (also known as Beal for Holy Island) was near the Holy Island causeway road. It opened in 1847 and was one of the few to stay open during the Second World War. The station closed to passengers on 29th January 1968. Postcard published by T. Henderson, Gavinton, Duns, Berwickshire.

69. Scremerston station, designed - as were many others in the area - by Newcastle architect Benjamin Green, opened on 29th March 1847 on the York, Newcastle and Berwick railway. Closed during the war, it was re-opened in 1946, only to close for good in July 1951.